CURTIS LEBLANC

BIRDING IN THE GLASS AGE OF ISOLATION

NIGHTWOOD EDITIONS

2020

Nightwood Editions
P.O. Box 1779
Gibsons, BC VON 1V0
Canada
www.nightwoodeditions.com

COVER PHOTOGRAPH: Kathryn Prescott
COVER DESIGN & TYPOGRAPHY: Carleton Wilson

Nightwood Editions acknowledges the support of the Canada Council for the Arts, the
Government of Canada, and the Province of British Columbia through the BC Arts Council.

This book has been produced on 100% post-consumer recycled, ancient-forest-free paper,
processed chlorine-free and printed with vegetable-based dyes.

Printed and bound in Canada.

LIBRARY AND ARCHIVES CANADA CATALOGUING IN PUBLICATION

Title: Birding in the glass age of isolation / Curtis LeBlanc.
Names: LeBlanc, Curtis, author.
Description: Poems.
Identifiers: Canadiana (print) 20190201177 | Canadiana (ebook) 20190201207 |
    ISBN 9780889713680 (softcover) | ISBN 9780889713697 (ebook)
Classification: LCC PS8623.E32775 B57 2020 | DDC C811/.6—dc23

TABLE OF CONTENTS

Part Three

In a pine tree,
A few yards from my window sill
A brilliant blue jay is springing up and down, up and
                              down,
On a branch.
I laugh, as I see him abandon himself
To entire delight, for he knows as well as I do
That the branch will not break.

– James Wright

PART ONE

It is one of those
common bodies that felt it could not exist without loving,
but has in fact gone on and on without love.

– CD Wright

FRANKENFISH

All the stormwater ponds in my hometown are overrun by giant goldfish, insatiable as teenagers demanding new love over and over, going from bus stop to bus stop eating everything they can afford with their grocery-store cheques and sliding-scale allowances.

I've been a sucker for the tragedy of memory, snuck into the beachtown kids' bingo tournament, slipped the neighbour boy a five to buy contraband cards to play with. I won an orange foam football on a vertical line and claimed my kid was back in bed, told the caller this is what he would've wanted.

That's all this is. Beer drunk from an inconspicuous coffee cup at the picnic table of a pitch-dark summer. Fresh crab caught between two tennis racquets, underbellies bashed in with the handle of a hairbrush. Dreams of planes emergency landing in the streets of Manhattan as we collect our bags and go for coffee after.

I'm twenty-six, overrun with the impossibility of ebbing back to Ker-Plunk or pick-up sticks. Drinking Canadian Club in an empty soccer field minutes before lightning. Climbing elementary school roofs for a better view. Holding an almost-stranger's soft hand while birds of prey scan the lake for fresh catch.

Today, in St. Albert, Alberta, they're poisoning the ponds with rotenone. Public works will scoop the dead with tiny nets into buckets. The official statement reads: *Any future regretful owners are to return their pets to the point of sale, or else kill and bury them.* Fine if the past won't take me back. But I want to live.

ON SEEING MY FATHER IN BRUEGEL'S *WINTER LANDSCAPE WITH SKATERS AND A BIRD TRAP*

He's the one who told me how he gathered
his skates and, like any kid with lips for lying,
told his mother he was meeting friends.
He walked five blocks to the Sturgeon River
to glide, alone, from Perron Street to the trestle
bridge. His feet, steel reeds caught in a current
of his own making. In Bruegel, he might see
himself, but not in the skaters, together
with arms linked, gliding on the green pond
of a place nothing like the one he suffered in.
He's in the birds, grounded, about to croak
beneath the wooden deadfall. Unhappiness,
a solid sheet dropping often on top of him.

                              Even in Bruges,
before he idled the rental in the street to relieve
himself in a café we had no intention of sitting
in, he and I found a way to be unhappy together.
It was our sleight-of-hand trick, a father
of absolutes and a son stuck in liminal splits.
The best photo I ever took of him: in anger,
cussing me out in the shadow of the Belfry,
that famous bell tower. He was somehow more
himself that way, finally spilling over the lip
of his unacceptable demureness, mostly quietude
and kindness in the body of a man at odds
with the men who held themselves above him.

Father, I have become you, some small shape
in the foreground, bracing myself for another
record winter and waiting for the sky to fall.

BIRDING IN THE GLASS AGE OF ISOLATION

Whoever said *kill* to a young boy
first is probably to blame
for this shotgun settled on my shoulder,

barrel pointed to the sky above my back.
Earlier we blasted a robin's-egg-blue
recliner to strips, waiting on breakfast.

Hangover sweat collects in the bottoms
of our gumboots. We're set to shoot
ourselves a grouse—

haven't even seen one yet—but we heard
how the blood dripped from the chin
of Dan's white bichon frise

after it got into the entrails of a fresh
roadside kill near the neighbour's
barbed-wire fence.

Nick, camera hung like a kettle bell
around his neck, tells me the two best
birders in Edmonton never leave

their minivan. Not until a bay-breasted
warbler or a northern goshawk
has been identified as perching

on a branch. We bushwhack into Crown
land at the south edge of Jared's Flatbush
ranch. In the bare wafer-board shack:

German pulp westerns, *The Glass Bees*
by Ernst Jünger, interspersed with smut
on the shelves of tenants past.

Man-made pond dyed a deep green
to keep algae from blooming, escaped
rabbits remembered by fur caught

in the chicken wire of their cages.
Smartphone held high, Nick repeats
a mating song with his Bird Calls app.

Be still, he says, and listen for the *clack-
clack, clack-clack*. Spruce grouse
will be on the forest bed, but taste

like the bitter red buds they're named for.
Ruffies, with their rumpled black necks,
gorge themselves on clover.

I'm out of focus, feeling it again,
a fugue I haven't felt since I smoked
Sage of the Diviners in undergrad,

lost a second summer to derealization
and my first clean hard hat.
The trees are a thick mesh screen,

the sky a steep slide to vertigo
and I feel it's best I shut my mouth
rather than explain this, gun in hand.

Jared raises his twenty-two, takes a crack
at another squirrel to sell to a man
who makes keychains from their tails,

but misses high again. It's almost noon.
I let a hare off easy. We're the renewed
embodiment of that old debate:

shoot to miss or capture in a high-res
image file, and what makes who
the better man? The sun slips behind

low clouds and I am no cooler for it.
I hear the love songs of smaller creatures,
clear as the day they were recorded,

sung again from the phone speaker's
shallow diaphragm. I want to lie down
on hard ground, rest my medicated head

on lichen-cuffed roots and list
all the times I allowed myself to want
without trying. I want to try.

FILMOGRAPHY OF MY EIGHTEENTH YEAR

There was a time
when in every picture
I am touching
my thumb to my lips
like Belmondo
or Seberg. I was trying
to say, *I'm breathless.*
I was trying to say,
I love you
through a thousand
cellar doors.

I spent my afternoons
in a hot tub alone,
a backyard
buried in snow.
When sickness set in,
I couldn't watch movies
anymore. One blue
period dissolved
into another, scored
by a wedding band.

Isn't it strange with memory,
how we can always say,
I was happy then?

A RESTAURANT IN CALIFORNIA

Everything I know about flight
I learned two hundred metres
below the surface of the earth.

In the belly of the Wapiti gravel
pit, the model rockets we fired
at the sun, lost for seconds

to the blinding blue, only to pop
their parachutes at the engine's
mid-flight burnout.

Some caught wind drifts,
decorated the tips of pine trees,
out of reach. Others malfunctioned,

a stray bead of the glue we dared
each other to huff left to harden
between fuselage and nose cone.

Such a waste, the ones that plummet
down into piles of rock, cardboard
uncoiling, crumpling into themselves.

Cole, you were so convinced
they could be fixed, gathering up
the refuse of busted fins.

Such was your optimism
that when, the following weekend,
your eight-month-old malamute

was stolen right from the garage,
you took out an ad in the paper
and pleaded for her safe return.

We saw each other again at twelve,
ate at the kids' table in a San Diego
bistro. You had hot wings

with blue cheese. I can still see
the white sauce dripping down
your chin, your bright orange

fingertips like batons guiding a pilot
safely in, as you told me how
a week went by before—chewing

gum matted in her fur—your dog
was returned to your garage
unscathed. If I could crash back

down into any moment, Cole,
I would let you marshal me down,
break through the clay-tile

roof of that restaurant in California
and hear again how it's possible for
some good to come if you ask for it.

SLAVE LAKE EPITHALAMIUM

I nearly lost my right foot
in the passenger seat of a golf cart

when Matthew drove up
the wheelchair ramp of the Winks

with my leg sticking out the side door.
It clacked like the ticker

of a spin wheel, from slat to white
wooden slat. My shoes were ruined,

my bones bruised, my body
a prop for cringe comedy.

STUBBORN PROPERTIES

after Natalie Shapero

I'm using a Band-Aid as a bookmark, Natalie,
reading the poems in *Hard Child*,
thinking about all the times I nearly gave up
my ghost as a kid because it was hard
to imagine the shortcomings of my physical body
could ever keep me from all the hot air
I saw as necessary. I tried so hard to win
a go-kart race, I took a too-fast turn
and crashed through the rubber tire meridian
and into the red dust and cacti of the Badlands.
Refused to let my friends question my grit,
stuck it out in an inner tube on the Pembina River
in sheets of rain and September temperatures
near freezing. When the campsite came into view,
where the Lobstick flows to Lake Chip,
I got out early and started walking. We fought
for warmth around the fire, hands so cold
I couldn't touch my pinky to my thumb,
but they still called me a coward for landing.
Worse still was driving the Coquihalla
with Alex, my pupils constricted to black pencil
tips, my sickness a whirlpool of static and colour
from the mountainsides around me.
I ignored the green jet streams that marbled
my periphery, held fast to the black singularity
of the road. We yelled along with the stereo,
untouchable and angry, a day's drive from home.

DESIGN STAGE FAILURE ANALYSIS

> *… a cage where a gerbil*
> *was kept, fed, to piss and quiver*
>
> *under a stunned boy's*
> *gaze until it ran itself out on the wheel.*
>
> – Ken Babstock

A pebble shot straight back
from the last on the left
of eighteen seething tires

into the windshield of an
unsuspecting traveller. Ensuing
crack in a perfect pane,

the birth of a false tributary,
compromised integrity
left unchecked to spread

until the odometer has finally
stopped dead. Banished
to the batting cage, a nucleus

of cork orbited by bleached
cowhide and red yarn, flung
from a rubber wheel to break

young wrists at Fall Ball
tryouts in September. An auger
that carves a perfect cylinder

through ice to fresh pike,
but can't reseal the wound,
complete the procedure.

A golden barrel cactus
that drinks itself top-heavy
then falls from the clay pot

to the floor. A Pygmalion
sculpture of boyhood hunger.
An engine with no choke.

UNFORGIVING AIR, ARUNDEL, QUEBEC

We were breath inside the rubber
mattresses that held our bodies
above the floorboards. We filled
the fridge and emptied it, La Fin
du Monde, Cinquante, Cheval Blanc,
and traced borders of the par-three
fairway with piss after dark.
We were as harsh as halogen
when the groundskeeper chased
us off. We were fireflies
having come of age in a place
too cold and dry for anything
as beautiful as fireflies. We were
marshland past the greenhouse
where larvae fed and formed
wings that allowed them to hover
against the backdrop of a blue-
black sky as we fed on their light.
We were cigarillos and toonie
scratch cards, not old enough to
own ourselves. We were currency.
We held our value only at night.
We were Autoroute 15 to Montreal
and the flatbed trucks that passed
while we ate at a casse-croûte
on the roadside. We were hands
that squished steamed hot dog
buns, salt that brined the cabbage
to choucroute, and when a drunk
driver lost the road and took

the whole shack out, we were
debris spread across the gravel lot.
We were cracks that compromised
the Canadian Shield, soft silt
and sediment pressed together
to form the rock that peaked above
the water's surface at Lac à la Loutre.
We back stroked to it and stood
knee-deep, panting and forever.
With bare hands we pulled small fish
into a world we swore was ours.
Into unforgiving air, we named them
in a language we didn't understand.

FAIR OAKS SUMMER

It was a kindness to leave the basement after days
of nature documentaries, to spread a yellow quilt
on the damp grass and kiss each other hastily.

Ants crept along our ankles on their way to sip
from clear droplets of water. Our youth, an itch
soothed by free time and sunlight.

My capacity for love was a raspberry beer
exploding after too long in the freezer. A part of me
is still asleep in the spare room of that summer,

afraid of the ache of being elsewhere. I'll tell you
now, I spent those long days perfectly on fire,
bare legs against the black leather interior.

POPLARS

There are times I am bothered
by the presence of my own body,
the toe that digs its jagged nail into
the larger toe, the leg that aches
in the stillness of night. At home,
the poplars that line the city streets
drop white cotton seeds like a blizzard
in the brightness of June. They gather
in drifts for neighbourhood kids
to use as kindling for brush fires.
Here, trees drop black sap that bakes
onto the hoods of parked cars,
becoming one with their enamel
until they return to the earth
in a junkyard or field. I don't know
what to make of that comparison
except to say I miss softness,
how it once gathered at my feet,
how rarely it gathers for me now.

MY BROTHER, FREE WILLY, PARIS 2013

In the Champs de Mars, my brother
and I chain-smoke bootlegged cigarettes,
Marlboro Reds touched together, fused
in heat like the scaffolding slats
of the Eiffel Tower to our left, tips
burning slow while the Gendarmerie
floodlights blind and glow over
the Facebook privacy rights protest
that we're taking in on our last night
in Paris. In the cab ride back to our flat,
the driver's pad of paper in the cupholder
reads   I AM   I AM HAPP
which is as close as I also ever get.
I can't speak for my brother who won't
tell me anything about himself until years
later, after we've gained a continent
and several Christmases between each
other. I know I like nothing
as much as he liked killer whales,
black backs breaching the blue bubble
television screen in our family's basement.
In what was once our favourite movie, Willy
puts his own face through the window
of his tank, he wants so badly to be free.

DON'T SWING

Fastball, curveball, changeup or breaker—
whatever left the hand of the pitcher—
as a child they told my father, *Don't swing.*
Don't swing to the Everclear drinkers
in the bathrooms at the Catholic junior high
school dance, or those who dared to hold
each other closer than the principal's
wooden ruler. Don't swing to the kids
who haunt the 7-Eleven parking lot, cemetery
of spent peach Prime Times and forties,
the others asleep beneath plastic stars
in their windowless basement bedrooms.
Don't swing to the school-hall firework lighters,
to the fire alarm pullers, to the front porch
shit burners and doorbell ringers, and to those
who still call to say good night. To those
who walk home together and alone,
to the ones who never make it home,
to the Snake Hill smokers and the Boudreau
bombers on cruisers and shortboards.
Don't swing to the singers in the bands
with their pawnshop teles, breathing life
into the basement of the Fraternal Order
of the Eagles Hall, to Mitch and all the others
who gave their lives for eight dollars
and fifty cents an hour. To Chris,
whose good was not a waste. To the ones
who love, endlessly and unashamed.
Don't swing. Don't swing.

WILD BLUEBERRY PIE

In eight weeks I'll be married, but first
I need to escape what this prairie heat
can do. Airport security won't let me board
with barbecue rub, and the forest-fire haze
has my flight delayed until further notice.
All weekend I burned like citronella oil
dumped freely on a bonfire, like the fuses
of crossettes and miniature bottle rockets,
like planks of pine cut crooked and left
for firewood at Old Joel's gravel drive.
His wife has misplaced all recollection
of her life. What's left will be spent
at a care centre in Westlock forty-five
minutes away. It was just last July
she took Joel's truck while he laboured
for leisure in his sawmill shed, went
into town to gather ingredients for pie
made from the wild blueberries
that give black bears the shits in shelterbelts
that keep the wind from turning the soil
loose and dry. Upon returning, she prepared
the dough, kneaded lard and flour
with the pronunciations of her white hands,
and combined berries, sugar and water
to boil down to sweetness. You think
you know what happens next. She slides
the pie into the oven, loses that near-frayed
twine in her mind that ties her moments
together, and returns to bed. Black smoke
never billowed from the oven door's

rubber seams. Alarms did not cut
that afternoon in two. The woman
was not reduced to ash with the house
while her husband sawed shoddy boards
from pines that fall silently like shooting
stars in the woods north of the pasture.
No, he returned inside for a drink
of water, found the pie and removed it,
golden at its edge. To think I have wanted
to forget so much of everything I've known.
I have considered, too, how unbearable
that would be. I imagine I will go on
this way, wishing and worrying
simultaneously, until the world
inevitably turns on me.

AT THE END OF THE FISCAL YEAR

There were desks and desks for me
to put the crowbar through so no one
else could possibly have a use for them.
Beside the garbage bin in the loading
bay of the business supplies department
store, I destroyed the smooth surfaces
that mocked maple and mahogany, oak

and pine, until they showed themselves
for who they really were: wood chips
and sawdust pressed into the semblance
of a solid sheet, the real thing. I was
a quiet kind of afraid, paid to break
apart the useless shit surrounding me.
I tapped my wisdom teeth together—

still seething just below my gums—
along to the beat of an imaginary drum
like I was watching my favourite band
play live for the first time in the church
basement, or the backroom of a place
I was still too young to be in. I killed
all idle time with kids who dumpster

dived at the bankrupt Burger King
across the street, crawled through
the colourful plastic of the dismantled
playroom. We bought fluorescent light
bulbs just to smash them on each other's
backs—white powdered ghosts to haunt
our cotton crewneck sweaters.

All I ever wanted was to feel at peace
in the company of others. Had you told
me it would take years, and that for some
it wouldn't come at all, I'd have never
left the loading bay, satisfied destroying
writeoffs that my weekend supervisor
had placed, like gifts, in front of me.

AXE HEAD

At eighteen, a rare alpine rain. I overflow into the dark of Stoney Creek,
feed the Battle River south. Hours earlier, she runs her fingers
on my skin past my waist beneath her grandmother's quilted duvet.
With her hand piloting mine, I do the same and wash my hands.

Firelight and a fifth of vodka. A blurry amble to the lakeside adult dance.
On the back steps of the amphitheatre, we buy pot from two guys with crowns
of moths and golden light, suck smoke from a plastic water-bottle pipe.
For the first time I am acrid when I piss myself and wash my hands.

At the office depot where I work, a woman is looking for a safe
to hide her medication and her money from her daughter. I climb
the ladder, pull the display box. Avoid her eyes as I dust it off.
Ask if there's anything else I can help with and wash my hands.

A blessed quarter-hour break. I bring the first aid kit to the toilet,
lock the stall and sit inside. With a safety pin and alcohol, I pick and rinse,
pick and rinse to erase the botched kitchen tattoo job on my thigh.
Blood smears like finger paint. I give up and wash my hands.

I want you to understand that in my sickness each denial was a marine
battery tied to my feet as I walked out into Fork Lake and a metaphor
made near-literal had I believed them not believing me. Instead I stand there
ankle deep in dusk's troubled light. Cast my shad and wash my hands.

There is no graffiti on American railcars, Grandpa tells me as we wait
for the new alfalfa-green containers featuring his late wife's favourite flower.
When the tiger lilies pass he claims she passes too, but I've never been
a believer of my grandma in the ether. I roll the window and wash my hands.

Our parents feared the bomb being dropped but we're afraid of growing up
so we purge a morning argument with the Jeopardy teen tournament, play best-
of-seven Yahtzee over beer and instant ramen. In the bathtub, I trim her hair.
At her feet, black thorns collect. She rinses off and I wash my hands.

I want to tell you exactly what I mean. I have split the wood of my youth,
over and over, looking for a grain I can at least recognize. Then this morning
I awoke in awe of the world, of these breaths I'm allowed to take
from it, and of you. I write this poem and wash my hands.

PART TWO

Sufferers [of hallucinogen persisting perception disorder (HPPD)] can appreciate that their perceptual aberrations are unreal—that their surroundings only appear blurred by afterimages (palinopsia) and trails (akinetopsia); shimmered by sparkles and flashed by bright bolts of light; interrupted by transparent blobs of color floating around; electrified by visual snow; magnified or shrunk by "Alice-in-Wonderland" symptoms; adorned by halos around objects, around people's heads.

– Dorian Rolston, *The New Yorker*, May 2013

MICROPSIA

A banner tied between
two trees on the shoulder
of the shrinking highway
to Fork Lake reads,

When prosperity ends,
real faith can begin, but
I have never felt smaller
and still don't believe
I will ever get better.

MACROPSIA

In bed for days on end
between workweeks
at the dig site. I spin
my head to see the red

digits stretch into the future,
past the alarm clock.
Each kernel of the popcorn
ceiling exploding into
catastrophe above me.

DEPERSONALIZATION

A bike of hornets builds a nest:
an abandoned car, an eave, a shed,
a mask of spit and paper.

DEREALIZATION

Lost in an empty room
with everyone you know.

FLOATERS

Fireflies.
Fruit flies.
Pop flies.
Flitter.

FALSE PERCEPTIONS OF MOVEMENT

Garden gnomes.
Mannequins.
Coat racks.
Scarecrows.

VISUAL SNOW

Sand dunes
swallow boys
who think
they're brave
for being
climbers.

POSITIVE AFTERIMAGES

I've seen my nightmares spill over
from my sleep and into my room
like water from a rising river:

                    a woman
perched on the edge of my bed,
her weight ebbing into the covers.

TRAILS

From sky to horizon where lightning touches the ground.
From the edge of the windshield after hitting the crow.
From the apartment I hated to the place we first met.
Down your neck and your shoulders to the pool of your back.

HALOS

Before the beautiful young people I knew
began to accidentally die, I didn't need
a path to the clearing of my mother's heaven,
only knowledge of a destination intended.

PART THREE

She's had less time
than some to learn the horse-like unpredictability of love.

– Ellie Sawatzky

A PRAIRIE MEASURE

You are a necklace of bees
like I am ten and standing on the lawn
of my great-grandmother's

Spy Hill home. All I know to be true
is the white whir of sound
from a wooden train whistle,

a gift from a time in my life
when all things were given to me.
A train passes, a prairie measure

of forever. A wasp lands on my hand,
but I know it won't sting me,
not now anyway, not in this memory.

SECOND SUMMER

John knew the two juniors
who broke into the house in Camrose,
the guys who didn't steal a thing,
but microwaved the tabby cat.

Lily knew the one who acted alone,
knew him to do most things alone.
Graduated into the lonely refineries
and liquor stores of Strathcona,
shot dead the four armed guards
and robbed the open Brink's truck.

Nathan knew who dished the licks
to Steve with a sawed-off goalie stick
behind the Shell—all our asses
blasted purple in the twilight
of our freshman August.

We thought we knew who took
a shit on the hood of Brenda's car.
Patrick knew him, wasn't surprised
when they found the pictures,
the kind whose existence on
its own is enough to make you cry.

No one had proof, but people claimed
they knew who wrote out the date
of the rumoured school massacre
on the boys' room toilet stall.
Many even thanked the kid
when we all got the day off
and went skating out at Grosvenor.

Ali knew something was up
when three guys gathered
in the doorway. Brandon busted in
and cut the other boy nine times,
right in front of her, at her feet.

From Akinsdale to Erin Ridge,
all through that second summer
when the city considered a curfew
and the Hollins kid got curb
stomped, all the adults asked us:
Where were you? Where were you?
Where were you? Where?

YOUR GRANDFATHER, AFTER WHIPPLE SURGERY

for Ken Maaker

Two at a time we went to watch him dying.
I held my hands in the waiting room while you
went in with your mother, the unit too narrow
for an audience. All around me: visitors,
Hawkins Cheezies, Tim Hortons' honey crullers.
I told you he wouldn't die and believed it
until I was called to the ICU where he lay,
swollen, a breathing tube, too heavy with pain
relievers to draw a picture or write a sentence.
He saw me, motioned me over and slipped
a hand between the buttons of my shirt.
The nurse dabbed his lips with cold water
while he moved his fingers along my stomach.
Death requires entirely new definitions of grace.

PHOTOGRAPH OF PÉPÈRE AFTER SHOOTING
A BLACK BEAR

You sit outside your canvas tent,
the corpse of a bear cocked up
and animated by flimsy sticks. You stare
at something far beyond the camera's
opal lens, slouching, pathetic rifle
at your side, its stock in the prized
black dirt. The kill was not a point
of pride, sport or contempt. Just
something you thought you had to do.
You came from Chatham, Minnesota
with your father to these plains.
They tried to reject you like a shard
of green glass. Had your father
stayed away, his wife may have never
caught the Spanish flu with her sister
inside those same two weeks.
Maybe Mémère might have remembered
my name at the Youville Home,
though I was too afraid to visit
as she lost all names to sickness
and age. Gonzo Burger might have
never closed and your children's
children could have swam the Sturgeon.
Maybe there would still be sawgrass
to blow on the one forgiving slope
where the hills number seven now
and they made you your grave.

OVER TIME

Me plus my mother equals greenhouse marigolds
    and a spade to break spring thaw.

Me plus my father equals silence
    and a poem made of office supplies.

Me plus my sister equals the tidal demise
    of a sandcastle empire.

Me plus my brother equals solitude
    in Orange County.

Me plus you equals the couches pushed together
    and thoughts of death subsided.

THE MELTING

Alone again, waiting for baby back ribs
to dethaw so I can rub them dry.
About that slip: to dethaw would be
to freeze again, and I haven't wanted that
since the summer I spent wasting,
waiting for my mind to solidify again.
Moments before denying my condition,
the doctor told me derealization is our way
of vacationing from a life too confusing
or painful to live. And yet the effect
is one of awareness, picking up
on exactly what's gone wrong and then
mourning it like a dead pet. Back then,
all I saw was melting, my mind a mosquito,
helpless to the last bright bulb left, hunting
drunk and hungry for the worst of it.

CAREER APTITUDE

We must've died a hundred times
or more on the battlefield
in your basement, prone in the couch-
cushion trenches of our collective
imagination. At seven, I wanted
to be a soldier, a general infantryman.
I sketched myself dealing death
on the back page of my first-grade
journal jacket. Then you pitched
us opening a custom auto body shop
while we were both sprawled out
on the Berber carpet, dead again
after a phantom raid too thick
for our platoon of two. I read *Motor
Trend* and *Road & Track*
and understood less than half.
Your brother grew into a heavy-duty
mechanic, worked long days beneath
the oil drips of backhoes and dozers.
He convinced you to use your head
and become an engineer instead.
At seventeen, I started up a punk
band. You went to draw thick
bitumen from the tar sands in Fort Mac.
On your week off, you flew home
to watch us play at the Pawnshop.
I broke a string and my strap slipped
off but you still said we *killed it.*

Now you're sleeping underground
where not even I can make a sound,
and for that I'm sorry.

ELECTION

I found my new America
passing out on the apartment floor,
shirt hanging open, counting
the hairs on my arms.

RIP BRADY FISCHER

I cared deeply for days
at the Christopher Robin's Nest
daycare between the dentist's
office and the gas station,
waited by the window for my mother
to pick me up on her way back
from bookkeeping
at the diamond cutter's.
I learned that seafood casserole
has no place in a landlocked
province, that one day I would be
old enough to care for children,
and if I chose to, it would make me
quick to anger and slow
to answer the cries. October,
I beat on circuit boards
and engines with a flathead
screwdriver and hammer
while others constructed
a haunted house with a cardboard
graveyard, RIP *Brady Fischer* across
every tombstone and mausoleum
door. Their way of saying,
We all wish you were dead.

POEM FOR GABRIELLE

I tried to teach you to roll your *Rs*
as we rolled along in the candy-apple red
Dodge Caravan to the French immersion
elementary school where *Rs* rolled
often without you, children growling
like small dogs at each other in pastel
blue halls. Your infant eyes were crossed,
lost in the space between near and far.
You were born with a hole through
the wall that divides your heart, blue
and red mixing like purple Kool-Aid
in the bendy straws of your blood
vessels, your body a series of dial tones
and jagged lines in a bed at the cardiologist's.
Once I hid behind the fence in our yard
and tried to scare your heart steady.
You ran around the house twice,
screaming, and most days now I wish
I could do the same. You got bifocals
that clipped tight behind your head,
and your tongue found the spot behind
your front teeth where it could rumble
through the dialect. Your chest
murmured along, like the beat of a song.

PHOSPHOROUS

The man in front of the menswear shop
mops the red-tile sidewalk outside
his door during the last cracks of January.

Steam stretches from the streaks of his labour
like ghost-coloured silly putty.

If all of this results in ice, if I slip
and tumble backward, will you make a basket
with your sweater and catch me?

It's morning and I'm on my way to work,
though I would have stayed
in the garden of our bed forever.

PÉPÈRE'S PUNCH

I am trying. I am trying to write.
I am trying to write a poem.

I am trying to write a poem
about Pépère bootlegging grain

liquor, bottles left for clandestine
pickup on range-road fence posts

around his farm in Beaumont,
borrowing the idea from Maurice,

a self-described black sheep,
his younger brother,

who smuggled up the Alaskan
Highway to labourers in dry camps.

It's what some might call
a heroic act, and I would too

if I were bound to a life under
rule of moderation in a place

so unforgivably cold and full
of ghosts. It's true I once found

love there, though I failed
to call it that before it up and left.

I've seen the northern lights
ruin a perfectly dark sky

and slept in fields of fresh cut
grass. I've cried myself

short of breath on strangers'
back porches, shaking

uncontrollably in the arms
of people whose names and faces

I forget. If you showed me
a clear path home, I'd call bullshit.

There are miles of young
mountains and highways frozen

between us. It's been a short life
so far and I already know too much.

NOTES

Poems from this book have previously appeared in *Grain, PRISM international, Poetry Is Dead, EVENT, Prairie Fire, The Fiddlehead, Arc* and *SAD,* and have been shortlisted for *CV2*'s Young Buck Poetry Prize. Thank you to the editors of each.

The opening epigraph is from James Wright's "Two Hangovers." The epigraph for Part One is from CD Wright's "Provinces." The epigraph for Part Two is from "A Trip That Doesn't End" by Dorian Rolston, an article published on *The New Yorker* website May 17, 2013. The epigraph for Part Three is from Ellie Sawatzky's "This Little Girl Goes to Burning Man." The epigraph for "Design Stage Failure Analysis" is from Ken Babstock's poem "Sawteeth."

The poem "Stubborn Properties" is after Natalie Shapero's poem "Hard Child."

ACKNOWLEDGEMENTS

Thank you to the team at Nightwood Editions and Harbour Publishing for their hard work, especially Amber McMillan, Silas White, Carleton Wilson, Nathaniel G. Moore and Marisa Alps.

A huge thank you to Adèle Barclay, Domenica Martinello and Jacob McArthur Mooney for their kind words and generosity, and to Kathryn Prescott for the perfect cover photograph.

I will always be grateful to my family, Ann, Marcel, Gabrielle and Marc, for their love and encouragement. Same goes for my friends and chosen family back home.

Also, thank you to my friends from the writing community for their constant inspiration and support, especially Dominique Bernier-Cormier, Brandi Bird, Selina Boan, Kayla Czaga, Chris Evans, Rachel Jansen, Jessica Johns, Megan Jones, Mica Lemiski, Karina Palmitesta, Shaun Robinson, Ellie Sawatzky, Kyle Schoenfeld, Carter Selinger, Jocelyn Tennant and Bryce Warnes.

This book would not have been possible without the generous support of the Canada Council for the Arts and the British Columbia Arts Council.

To Mallory, the most gratitude I can possibly muster.

PHOTO CREDIT: ROSSANNE CLAMP

ABOUT THE AUTHOR

Curtis LeBlanc's debut collection, *Little Wild*, was published by Nightwood Editions in 2018. His poems have won the Readers' Choice Award in *Arc*'s Poem of the Year competition, honourable mention in the Margaret Reid Poetry Contest, and have been short-listed for *The Walrus* Poetry Prize and *CV2*'s Young Buck Poetry Prize. More of his work has appeared in *Geist, Prairie Fire, EVENT, PRISM international, Grain, The Literary Review of Canada, The Rusty Toque, Alberta Views, Poetry Is Dead* and elsewhere. He lives with his wife Mallory Tater in Vancouver, where they run Rahila's Ghost Press.